Ninja Foodi Grill Cookbook #2020

Affordable, Easy & Delicious Recipes for Indoor Grilling & Air

Frying | 21-Day Meal Plan

Larda Houter

Table of contents

Chapter 1: Understanding the Ninja foodi Grill

Ninja Foodi Grill is nothing but convenience for those who love to enjoy nicely grilled food but are too busy to set up an outdoor grill every now and then. It has brought innovation right at our fingertips by bringing all the necessary cooking options in a digital one-touch device. It is simple to manage and control. What makes the Ninja foodi grill stand apart from other electric grills is the diversity of options it provides for cooking all in a single pot. The ceramic coated interior and accessories make grilling an effortless experience. This cookbook puts the idea of the electric grill into perspective by discussing the basics of using the Ninja Foodi Grill. The company has launched the appliance with only one aim that is to provide convenient grilling for all. Try the flavorsome grilling recipes in your Ninja Food grill and experience good taste with amazing aromas, all with little efforts and in lesser time.

The Benefits of Using an Electric grill

Following are few of the known benefits that an electric grill like that of Ninja Foodi Grill guarantees to provide:

1. Temperature and Pressure Maintenance

The function of the rheostat and thermostat is to keep the internal temperature of the grill. As with charcoal grills, we are required to maintain it manually with a constant check, whereas in electric grills, the thermostat does that for us. In case of a rise in temperature beyond the set the limit, it automatically switches off its circuit to reduce the temperature.

2. Safe and Friendly

As in electric grill, you are not required to light any fire on your own; it is much less dangerous than other grills. The wiring is completely insulated, and the entire unit is protected with a solid layering on the outside. With a careful understanding of the device, the electric grills prove to be user-friendly and safe to use.

3. Energy Efficient

Many people believe that electric grills might add a lot to their electricity bills. Though these grills are reliant on electricity, yet they are energy efficient in this regard. About

1760 watts per hour of electricity is used while using an electric grill like Ninja Foodi Grill.

4. Lesser Pollution

Since these grills use electric energy, they are a more environment-friendly option then charcoal grills. The food is kept safe and free from the outer atmosphere and contaminants. As the food is cooked in a closed setting, its flavor is well preserved, and the moisture is not lost.

5. Easy to Use for Beginners

Previously it was known that only people with good cooking experience could deal with grills, but now with electric grills like Ninja Foodi, even beginners can cook like pros by following its manual and recipes.

Structural Composition of the Ninja foodi Grill

The advanced multifunctional 5 in one kitchen miracle Ninja Foodi Grill has made grilling an effortless experience. Who knew indoor grilling would become so easy to go someday? But now Ninja Foodi has introduced its mule purpose grill appliance, which allows you to grill, bake, roast, air fry, and dehydrate different food items. The device is available in different sizes and models. And each package comes with different accessories and money-back guarantee. How there are certain components which are commonly available in all of Ninja Food Grill models, as follows:

- Ninja® Foodi™ 5-in-1 Indoor Grill
- 4-Quart Air Fryer
- Grill, the air crisp, bake, roast,
- Dehydrate functions
- Virtually smoke-free
- Smoke Control Technology
- 6-quart ceramic-coated
- cooking pot
- 10" x 10" ceramic-coated grill
- grate
- 4-quart ceramic-coated crisper

- basket
- Kebab skewers (5 pack)
- Cleaning brush
- 20-recipe book
- 1-year VIP warranty
- 90-day money-back guarantee

When you unbox the appliance, you will find plenty of accessories along with the base unit. The base unit is an insulated vessel which has a flip lid attached to one side of the base. When you open the Food's lid, there is a hollow space inside for the cooking of the food. For that space firstly there is a cooking basket, an air fryer basket, a grill, a grate and a crisper. Based on the functions of the cooking these inner baskets are used, which will be discussed in the next section.

Outside the base unit, there is a digital control panel with LED screen at the center. The Screen displays the cooking temperature and internal temperature of the food plus when to add the food and when the device is preheated. Then there are buttons to select the preset temperature settings and to increase or decrease the cooking timings

The settings for cooking temperature are given as Low to Medium, to High, and to the Max. Each mode states a different temperature on the screen. The highest being the 510 degrees F. Whichever mode we select, the temperature is set accordingly. The timer button allows us to increase or decrease cooking timings as desired.

Chapter 2: How to Use the Ninja Foodi Grill

The use of the Ninja foodi grill gets easy if we divide the whole process into three basic steps: Assemble, Prepare, And Cook!'

Assemble

- For every session of cooking, you will need to assemble the device accordingly. First, clean the interior and exterior of the device with a clean cloth.
- Now plug in the device and press the power button to switch on the device.
- Open the lid of the Ninja Foodi Grill.
- Place the ceramic coated cooking pot inside the grill. This basket is removable and dishwasher safe.
- Now depending on the cooking mode: Select grill for grilling, air fryer basket for an air fryer, crisper plate for dehydrating and grate for baking roasting, etc. and place them in the ceramic coated cooking pot of the grill.
- Now the device is ready assembled.

Prepare

- The preparation steps include two basic things. Firstly, to grease the container of the cooking pot, whether it's the grill, grate, air fryer basket with a cooking spray to prevent food from sticking. It is a mandatory step, whether the recipe says it or not.
- Once the internal basket and its accessories are greased with cooking spray, it is time to preheat the device.
- Select the mode for cooking by pressing their respective button:
  1. Grilling
  2. Air Frying
  3. Baking
  4. Roasting
  5. Dehydrating
- For preheating, simply select any of the 4 desired temperature settings.
  1. Low: 400 F
  2. Medium: 450F
  3. High: 500 F

4.   Max: 510 F

- Now Select the time for cooking by pressing the increase or decrease button of the timer.
- Then cover the lid, now the device will start to preheat, and it will show the bars.
- It takes 8 minutes for the device to preheat completely, and this will show all the bars on the screen.
- Once the device is preheated, it automatically says to "Add Food" on the screen.
- Now open the lid and place the food inside of the hot grill.
- Insert the temperature probe into the meat to constantly detect the internal temperature.

Cook!

- To start the cooking, cover the lid of the grill, and it will start cooking.
- As we constantly need to flip the food during grilling, so we can easily open the lid, and it will automatically pause the cooking.
- The cooking will be resume once we close the lid again.
- Use the start and stop button to manually initiate and pause cooking.
- Check when the food's internal temperature reaches the desired level.
- Open the lid and remove the food to serve.

Remember that in a continuous session, the Ninja foodi might not take much time for preheating the second time as it would be already preheated from the first session.

Cleaning and Maintenance

All the accessories of the device are 100 percent dishwasher safe, so you can wash them easily in the dishwasher. Avoid scratching the accessories as it may damage the ceramic coating.

- After cooking, unplug the device and allow it to cool down first.
- Leave the lid open when the device is cooling down.
- Remove the inner grills or baskets and the cooking pot and remove if there are any solid food particles in it.
- Now you can either dish wash them carefully or wash them with soapy water to remove the grease.

- Allow all the accessories to dry before putting them back into the place.
- Use the brush given with the grill to scrap of all the grease. Avoid using other hard brushes to prevent any damage.
- Clean the base unit from inside and the outside using a lightly wet cloth.
- Do not immerse or wash the base unit or the lid with water.

Troubleshooting

- To avoid troubleshooting, a check is the cooking pot is not overly stuffed or loaded.
- Keep the food only up to 2/3 of the cooking pot's height and avoid overstuffing.
- Use only one grill or inner basket at a time.
- Check if the lid is properly closed before start cooking.
- If the device is physically damaged, do not continue cooking and instantly call for customer support.

Frequently asked questions

1. Which accessory to use for air frying purposes?

There is a separated air frying basket that comes with the grill, places this basket inside the cooking pot of the grill, and then put food in it for cooking.

2. Can I cook liquid food in the Grill's cooking pot?

The Ninja Foodi Grill is designed for grilling, air frying, and roasting purposes, cooking soups, stews, and other liquids inside the cooking pot is not appropriate. Stick to the Ninja Foodi Grill specific recipes.

3. Is preheating necessary before cooking?

Yes, this time is required by the device to reach the temperature at which you want to cook the food. Without preheating, the selected cooking time will not yield the desired results.

Chapter 3: Breakfast Recipes

Grilled Bruschetta

Prep Time: 10 minutes
Cooking Time: 8 minutes
Serving: 6

Ingredients

- 1 cup chopped celery
- 3 tablespoons Dijon mustard
- 1-lb. plum tomatoes, seeded and chopped
- 3 tablespoons balsamic vinegar
- 1/4 cup minced fresh basil
- 3 tablespoons olive oil
- 2 garlic cloves, minced
- 1/2 teaspoon salt

Spread:

- 1 tablespoon finely chopped green onion
- 1/4 cup Dijon mustard
- 1 garlic clove, minced
- 3/4 teaspoon dried oregano
- 1/2 cup mayonnaise
- 1 loaf French bread, sliced

Method:

1. Take the first eight ingredients in a bowl and mix them together.
2. Cover this prepared topping and refrigerate for about 30 minutes.
3. Now take mayonnaise, onion, garlic, oregano, and mustard in a bowl.
4. Mix them well and prepare the mayonnaise spread.
5. Prepare and preheat the Ninja Foodi Grill in the medium-temperature setting.
6. Once it is preheated, open the lid and place the bread slices on the grill in batches.

7. Cover the Ninja Foodi Grill's lid and let it grill on the "Grilling Mode" for 2 minutes.
8. Flip the bread slices and grill again for 2 minutes.
9. Top the grilled bread with mayonnaise spread and tomato relish.
10. Serve fresh.

Nutritional Information per Serving:

- Calories 284
- Total Fat 7.9 g
- Saturated Fat 1.4 g
- Cholesterol 36 mg
- Sodium 704 mg
- Total Carbs 46 g
- Fiber 3.6 g
- Sugar 5.5 g
- Protein 7.9 g

Grilled Chicken Tacos

Prep Time: 10 minutes
Cooking Time: 30 minutes
Serving: 8

Ingredients

- 2 tablespoons chipotle in adobo sauce, chopped
- 2 teaspoons sugar
- 1/3 cup olive oil
- 1/3 cup lime juice
- 1/3 cup red wine vinegar
- 2 teaspoons salt
- 2 teaspoons pepper
- 1 cup fresh cilantro, chopped
- 2 lbs. boneless skinless chicken thighs

Taco wraps:

- 8 flour tortillas
- 4 poblano peppers
- 1 tablespoon olive oil
- 2 cups shredded Jack cheese

Method:

1. Take the first six ingredients in a blender jug and blend them together.
2. Once blended, mix with chipotles and cilantro.
3. Mix chicken with this cilantro marinade and cover to refrigerate for 8 hours.
4. Grease the poblanos with cooking oil and keep them aside.
5. Prepare and preheat the Ninja Foodi Grill on a High-temperature setting.
6. Once it is preheated, open the lid and place the peppers in the grill.
7. Cover the Ninja Foodi Grill's lid and let it grill on the "Grilling Mode" for 2 minutes.
8. Flip the peppers and then continue grilling for another 2 minutes.
9. Its time to grill the chicken in the same grill.

10. Place the chicken in the grill and cover the lid.
11. Select the High-temperature setting on the Grill.
12. Ninja Grill the chicken for 5 minutes per side then transfers to a plate.
13. Now peel and slice the peppers in half then also slice the chicken.
14. Spread each tortilla and add half cup chicken, half peppers and ¼ cup cheese.
15. Fold the tortilla and carefully place in the grill and cover its lid.
16. Grill each for 2 minutes per side on the medium temperature setting.
17. Serve.

Nutritional Information per Serving:

- Calories 134
- Total Fat 4.7 g
- Saturated Fat 0.6 g
- Cholesterol 124mg
- Sodium 1 mg
- Total Carbs 54.1 g
- Fiber 7 g
- Sugar 3.3 g
- Protein 26.2 g

Grilled French Toast

Prep Time: 10 minutes
Cooking Time: 8 minutes
Serving: 3

Ingredients

- 3- 1-inch slices challah bread
- 2 eggs
- Juice of ½ orange
- ½ quart strawberries, quartered
- 1 tablespoon honey
- 1 tablespoon balsamic vinegar
- 1 teaspoon orange zest
- 1/2 sprig fresh rosemary
- ½ teaspoon vanilla extract
- Salt to taste
- 1/4 cup heavy cream
- Fine sugar, for dusting, optional

Method:

1. Spread a foil sheet on a working surface.
2. Add strawberries, balsamic, orange juice, rosemary, and zest.
3. Fold the foil edges to make a pocket.
4. Whisk egg with cream, honey, vanilla, and a pinch of salt.
5. Dip and soak the bread slices in this mixture and shake off the excess.
6. Prepare and preheat the Ninja Foodi Grill in the medium-temperature setting.
7. Once it is preheated, open the lid and place the bread slices and the foil packet on the grill.
8. Cover the Ninja Foodi Grill's lid and let them grill on the "Grilling Mode" for 2 minutes in batches.
9. Flip the bread slices and continue grilling for another 2 minutes.
10. Serve the bread with the strawberry mix on top.
11. Enjoy.

Nutritional Information per Serving:

- Calories 387
- Total Fat 6 g
- Saturated Fat 9.9 g
- Cholesterol 41 mg
- Sodium 154 mg
- Total Carbs 37.4 g
- Fiber 2.9 g
- Sugar 15.3 g
- Protein 14.6 g

Sausage with Eggs

Prep Time: 10 minutes
Cooking Time: 10 minutes
Serving: 4

Ingredients

- 4 sausage links
- 2 cups chopped kale
- 1 medium sweet yellow onion
- 4 eggs
- 1 cup mushrooms
- olive oil

Method:

1. Prepare and preheat the Ninja Foodi Grill in a High-temperature setting.
2. Once it is preheated, open the lid and place the sausages on the grill.
3. Cover the Ninja Foodi Grill's lid and let it grill on the "Grilling Mode" for 2 minutes.
4. Flip the sausages and continue grilling for another 3 minutes
5. Now spread the onion, mushrooms, and kale in an iron skillet.
6. Crack the eggs in between the sausages.
7. Bake this mixture for 5 minutes the oven at 350 degrees F.
8. Serve warm and fresh.

Nutritional Information per Serving:

- Calories 212
- Total Fat 11.8 g
- Saturated Fat 2.2 g
- Cholesterol 23mg
- Sodium 321 mg
- Total Carbs 14.6 g
- Dietary Fiber 4.4 g
- Sugar 8 g
- Protein 17.3 g

Espresso Glazed Bagels

Prep Time: 10 minutes
Cooking Time: 8 minutes
Serving: 4

Ingredients

- 4 bagels, split in half
- 1/4 cup coconut milk
- 1 cup fine sugar
- 2 tablespoons black coffee
- 2 tablespoons coconut flakes

Method:

1. Prepare and preheat the Ninja Foodi Grill on a medium-temperature setting.
2. Once it is preheated, open the lid and place 2 bagels in the grill.
3. Cover the Ninja Foodi Grill's lid and let it grill on the "Grilling Mode" for 2 minutes.
4. Flip the bagel and continue grilling for another 2 minutes.
5. Grill the remaining bagels in a similar way.
6. Whisk the rest of the ingredients in a bowl well.
7. Drizzle this sauce over the grilled bagels.
8. Serve.

Nutritional Information per Serving:

- Calories 412
- Total Fat 24.8 g
- Saturated Fat 12.4 g
- Cholesterol 3 mg
- Sodium 132 mg
- Total Carbs 43.8 g
- Dietary Fiber 3.9 g
- Sugar 2.5 g
- Protein 18.9 g

Bruschetta Portobello Mushrooms

Prep Time: 10 minutes
Cooking Time: 8 minutes
Serving: 6

Ingredients

- 2 cups cherry tomatoes, cut in half
- 3 tablespoons red onion, diced
- 3 tablespoons fresh basil shredded
- Salt and black pepper to taste
- 4 tablespoons butter
- 1 teaspoon dried oregano
- 6 large Portobello Mushrooms, caps only, washed and dried

Balsamic glaze:

- 2 teaspoons brown sugar
- 1/4 cup balsamic vinegar

Method:

1. Start by preparing the balsamic glaze and take all its ingredients in a saucepan.
2. Stir cook this mixture for 8 minutes on medium heat then remove from the heat.
3. Take the mushrooms and brush them with the prepared glaze.
4. Stuff the remaining ingredients into the mushrooms.
5. Prepare and preheat the Ninja Foodi Grill in the medium-temperature setting.
6. Once it is preheated, open the lid and place the stuffed mushrooms in grill with their cap side down.
7. Cover the Ninja Foodi Grill's lid and let it grill on the "Grilling Mode" for 8 minutes.
8. Serve.

Nutritional Information per Serving:

- Calories 331
- Total Fat 2.5 g

- Saturated Fat 0.5 g
- Cholesterol 35 mg
- Sodium 595 mg
- Total Carbs 69 g
- Fiber 12.2 g
- Sugar 12.5 g
- Protein 8.7g

Avocado Eggs

Prep Time: 10 minutes
Cooking Time: 5 minutes
Serving: 2

Ingredients

- 1 ripe avocado
- 1 pinch of barbecue rub
- 2 eggs
- Salt and pepper, to taste
- 1 red jalapeño, finely diced
- 1 tomato, chopped

Method:

1. Slice the avocado in half and remove its pit.
2. Remove some flesh from the center then crack an egg into the halves.
3. Drizzle barbecue rub, salt, pepper, jalapeno and tomato on top.
4. Prepare and preheat the Ninja Foodi Grill in a High-temperature setting.
5. Once it is preheated, open the lid and place the stuffed avocado in grill with their skin side down.
6. Cover the Ninja Foodi Grill's lid and let it grill on the "Grilling Mode" for 5 minutes.
7. Serve.

Nutritional Information per Serving:

- Calories 322
- Total Fat 11.8 g
- Saturated Fat 2.2 g
- Cholesterol 56 mg
- Sodium 321 mg
- Total Carbs 14.6 g
- Dietary Fiber 4.4 g
- Sugar 8 g
- Protein 17.3 g

Coconut French Toast

Prep Time: 10 minutes
Cooking Time: 16 minutes
Serving: 5

Ingredients

- 1/4 cup milk
- 3 large eggs
- 1 (12-oz.) loaf bread- 10 slices
- 1/4 cup sugar
- Cooking spray
- 1 cup of coconut milk
- 10 (1/4-inch-thick) slices pineapple, peeled
- 1/2 cup coconut flakes

Method:

1. Whisk the coconut milk with sugar, eggs, and fat-free milk in a bowl.
2. Dip the bread in this mixture and keep it aside for 1 minute.
3. Prepare and preheat the Ninja Foodi Grill on medium-temperature setting.
4. Once it is preheated, open the lid and place 5 bread slices on the grill.
5. Cover the Ninja Foodi Grill's lid and let it grill on the "Grilling Mode" for 2 minutes.
6. Flip the slices and continue grilling for another 2 minutes.
7. Cook the remaining 5 slices in a similar way.
8. Now grill 5 pineapples slices on the grill for 2 minutes per side.
9. Grill the remaining pineapple in the same way.
10. Serve the bread with pineapple on top.
11. Garnish with coconut and serve.

Nutritional Information per Serving:

- Calories 197
- Total Fat 15.4 g
- Saturated Fat 4.2 g

- Cholesterol 168 mg
- Sodium 203 mg
- Total Carbs 58.5 g
- Sugar 1.1 g
- Fiber 4 g
- Protein 7.9 g

Bacon-Herb Grit

Prep Time: 10 minutes
Cooking Time: 10 minutes
Serving: 4

Ingredients

- 1 tablespoon minced fresh
- 2 teaspoons chopped fresh parsley
- 1/2 teaspoon garlic powder
- 1/2 teaspoon black pepper
- 3 bacon slices, cooked and crumbled
- 1/2 cup shredded cheddar cheese
- 4 cups instant grits
- Cooking spray

Method:

1. Start by mixing the first seven ingredients in a suitable bowl.
2. Spread this mixture in a 10-inch baking pan and refrigerate for 1 hour.
3. Flip the pan on a plate and cut the grits mixture into 4 triangles.
4. Prepare and preheat the Ninja Foodi Grill in the medium-temperature setting.
5. Once it is preheated, open the lid and place the grit slices in the grill.
6. Cover the Ninja Foodi Grill's lid and let it grill on the "Grilling Mode" for 5 minutes per side.
7. serve

Nutritional Information per Serving:

- Calories 138
- Total Fat 9.7 g
- Saturated Fat 4.7 g
- Cholesterol 181 mg
- Sodium 245 mg
- Total Carbs 32.5 g
- Fiber 0.3 g
- Sugar 1.8 g
- Protein 10.3 g

Toast Kebabs

Prep Time: 10 minutes
Cooking Time: 6 minutes
Serving: 4

Ingredients

- 1 loaf (1 lb.) bread
- 3/4 cup milk
- 4 large eggs
- 1 teaspoon vanilla extract

Method:

1. Take all the ingredients in a suitable bowl except the loaf and mix well.
2. Dice the load into even-sized cubes.
3. Dip these cubes in the prepared mixture then thread on the skewers.
4. Prepare and preheat the Ninja Foodi Grill in a low-temperature setting.
5. Once it is preheated, open the lid and place the bread skewers on the grill.
6. Cover the Ninja Foodi Grill's lid and let it grill on the "Grilling Mode" for 2 minutes.
7. Turn the skewers and continue grilling for 2 minutes per side.
8. Serve.

Nutritional Information per Serving:

- Calories 391
- Total Fat 2.8 g
- Saturated Fat 0.6 g
- Cholesterol 330 mg
- Sodium 62 mg
- Total Carbs 36.5 g
- Fiber 9.2 g
- Sugar 4.5 g
- Protein 26.6

Chapter 4: Poultry

Chicken and Tomatoes

Prep Time: 10 minutes
Cooking Time: 12 minutes
Serving: 4

Ingredients

- 2 tablespoons olive oil
- 1 garlic clove, minced
- 1/2 teaspoon salt
- 1/4 cup fresh basil leaves
- 8 plum tomatoes
- 3/4 cup vinegar
- 4 chicken breast, boneless skinless

Method:

1. Take the first five ingredients together in a blender jug.
2. Blend them well then add four tomatoes to blend again.
3. Take chicken in a suitable bowl and pour 2/3 cup of the prepared marinade.
4. Mix well and refrigerate the chicken for 1 hour.
5. Prepare and preheat the Ninja Foodi Grill on a High-temperature setting.
6. Once it is preheated, open the lid and place the 2 chicken pieces on the grill.
7. Cover the Ninja Foodi Grill's lid and let it grill on the "Grilling Mode" for 3 minutes.
8. Flip the grilled chicken and continue grilling until it is al dente.
9. Cook the remaining chicken in a similar way.
10. Serve.

Nutritional Information per Serving:

- Calories 453
- Total Fat 2.4 g
- Saturated Fat 3 g

- Cholesterol 21 mg
- Sodium 216 mg
- Total Carbs 18 g
- Fiber 2.3 g
- Sugar 1.2 g
- Protein 23.2 g

Spinach Burgers

Prep Time: 10 minutes
Cooking Time: 64 minutes
Serving: 8

Ingredients

- 1 tablespoon avocado oil
- 2 shallots, chopped
- 2-1/2 cups fresh spinach, chopped
- 3 garlic cloves, minced
- 2/3 cup crumbled feta cheese
- 3/4 teaspoon Greek seasoning
- 1/2 teaspoon salt
- 1/4 teaspoon pepper
- 2 lbs. of turkey ground
- 8 hamburger buns, split

Method:

1. Start by sautéing shallots in a skillet for 2 minutes, then add garlic and spinach.
2. Cook for 45 seconds then transfers to a suitable bowl.
3. Add all the seasoning, beef, and feta cheese to the bowl.
4. Mix well then make 8 patties of ½ inch thickness.
5. Prepare and preheat the Ninja Foodi Grill on the medium temperature setting.
6. Once it is preheated, open the lid and place 2 patties on the grill.
7. Cover the Ninja Foodi Grill's lid and let it grill on the "Grilling Mode" for 8 minutes.
8. Flip the patties and continue grilling for another 8 minutes.
9. Grill the remaining patties in a similar way.
10. Serve the patties in between the buns with desired toppings.
11. Enjoy.

Nutritional Information per Serving:

- Calories 529

- Total Fat 17 g
- Saturated Fat 3 g
- Cholesterol 65 mg
- Sodium 391 mg
- Total Carbs 55 g
- Fiber 6 g
- Sugar 8 g
- Protein 41g

Chicken Sandwiches

Prep Time: 10 minutes
Cooking Time: 24 minutes
Serving: 4

Ingredients

- 1/4 cup reduced-fat mayonnaise
- 1 tablespoon Dijon mustard
- 1 tablespoon honey
- 4 chicken breasts, halves
- 1/2 teaspoon Montreal seasoning
- 4 slices Swiss cheese
- 4 hamburger buns, split
- 2 bacon strips, cooked and crumbled
- Lettuce leaves and tomato slices, optional

Method:

1. First, lb. the chicken with a mallet into ½ inch thickness.
2. Now season it with steak seasoning and rub it well.
3. Prepare and preheat the Ninja Foodi Grill on a medium temperature setting.
4. Once it is preheated, open the lid and place 2 chicken pieces on the grill.
5. Cover the Ninja Foodi Grill's lid and let it grill on the "Grilling Mode" for 6 minutes.
6. Flip the chicken and continue grilling for another 6 minutes.
7. Cook the remaining chicken in a similar way.
8. Mix mayonnaise with honey, and mustard in a bowl
9. Place the one chicken piece on top of each half of the bun.
10. Top it with mayo mixture, 1 cheese slices, and other toppings.
11. Place the other bun halve on top.
12. Serve.

Nutritional Information per Serving:

- Calories 284

- Total Fat 25 g
- Saturated Fat 1 g
- Cholesterol 49 mg
- Sodium 460 mg
- Total Carbs 35 g
- Fiber 2 g
- Sugar 6 g
- Protein 26g

Sriracha Wings

Prep Time: 10 minutes
Cooking Time: 10 minutes
Serving: 6

Ingredients

- 12 chicken wings
- 1 tablespoon canola oil
- 2 teaspoons ground coriander
- 1/2 teaspoon garlic salt
- 1/4 teaspoon pepper

Sauce/Glaze

- 1/2 cup orange juice
- 1/3 cup Sriracha chili sauce
- 1/4 cup butter, cubed
- 3 tablespoons honey
- 2 tablespoons lime juice
- 1/4 cup chopped fresh cilantro

Method:

1. Season the wings with all its seasoning in a suitable bowl.
2. Mix well then cover to refrigerate for 2 hours of marination.
3. Meanwhile, prepare the sauce by cooking its ingredients in a saucepan for 4 minutes.
4. Prepare and preheat the Ninja Foodi Grill on the medium temperature setting.
5. Once it is preheated, open the lid and place the chicken wings on the grill.
6. Cover the Ninja Foodi Grill's lid and let it grill on the "Grilling Mode" for 5 minutes.
7. Flip the grilled wings and continue cooking for another 5 minutes.
8. Drizzle the prepared sauce over the wings in a bowl.
9. Toss well and serve.

Nutritional Information per Serving:

- Calories 352
- Total Fat 14 g
- Saturated Fat 2 g
- Cholesterol 65 mg
- Sodium 220 mg
- Total Carbs 15.8 g
- Fiber 0.2 g
- Sugar 1 g
- Protein 26 g

Bourbon Drumsticks

Prep Time: 10 minutes
Cooking Time: 24 minutes
Serving: 3

Ingredients

- ½ cup ketchup
- 1 tablespoon brown sugar
- 2 teaspoon BBQ seasoning
- 6 chicken drumsticks
- 1 pinch teaspoon salt
- 1 tablespoon bourbon
- 1/3 cup Dr. Pepper spice seasoning
- ½ tablespoon Worcestershire sauce
- 1 teaspoon dried onion, chopped finely

Method:

1. Take the first eight ingredients in a saucepan.
2. Stir cook for 10 minutes on a simmer until the sauce thickens.
3. Prepare and preheat the Ninja Foodi Grill in a High-temperature setting.
4. Once it is preheated, open the lid and place 3 drumsticks in the grill and brush it with the sauce.
5. Cover the Ninja Foodi Grill's lid and let it grill on the "Grilling Mode" for 6 minutes.
6. Flip the grilled chicken and baste it with the remaining sauce.
7. Continue grilling for another 6 minutes until al dente.
8. Garnish with remaining sauce on top.
9. Serve.

Nutritional Information per Serving:

- Calories 388
- Total Fat 8 g
- Saturated Fat 1 g

- Cholesterol 153mg
- sodium 339 mg
- Total Carbs 8 g
- Fiber 1 g
- Sugar 2 g
- Protein 13 g

Tomato Turkey Burgers

Prep Time: 10 minutes
Cooking Time: 42 minutes
Serving: 6

Ingredients

- 1 large red onion, chopped
- 1 cup (4 oz.) feta cheese
- 2/3 cup sun-dried tomatoes, chopped
- 1/4 teaspoon salt
- 1/4 teaspoon pepper
- 2 lbs. lean ground turkey
- 6 ciabatta rolls, slice in half

Method:

1. Take all the ingredients for burgers in a bowl except the ciabatta rolls.
2. Mix well and make six patties out of this turkey mixture.
3. Prepare and preheat the Ninja Foodi Grill in the medium-temperature setting.
4. Once it is preheated, open the lid and place 2 turkey patties on the grill.
5. Cover the Ninja Foodi Grill's lid and let it grill on the "Grilling Mode" for 7 minutes.
6. Flip the patties and continue grilling for another 7 minutes.
7. Grill the remaining patties in a similar way.
8. Serve with ciabatta rolls.

Nutritional Information per Serving:

- Calories 301
- Total Fat 15.8 g
- Saturated Fat 2.7 g
- Cholesterol 75 mg
- Sodium 189 mg
- Total Carbs 31.7 g
- Fiber 0.3 g
- Sugar 0.1 g
- Protein 28.2 g

Chicken with Grilled Apples

Prep Time: 10 minutes
Cooking Time: 18 minutes
Serving: 4

Ingredients

- 4 chicken breasts, halved
- 4 teaspoons chicken seasoning
- 1 large apple, wedged
- 1 tablespoon lemon juice
- 4 slices provolone cheese
- 1/2 cup Alfredo sauce
- 1/4 cup crumbled blue cheese

Method:

1. Take chicken in a bowl and season it with chicken seasoning.
2. Toss apple with lemon juice in another small bowl.
3. Prepare and preheat the Ninja Foodi Grill in the medium-temperature setting.
4. Once it is preheated, open the lid and place the chicken in the grill.
5. Cover the Ninja Foodi Grill's lid and let it grill on the "Grilling Mode" for 8 minutes approximately.
6. Flip the grilled chicken and continue cooking for another 8 minutes.
7. Now grill the apple in the same grill for 2 minutes per side.
8. Serve the chicken with apple, blue cheese, and alfredo sauce.
9. Enjoy.

Nutritional Information per Serving:

- Calories 231
- Total Fat 20.1 g
- Saturated Fat 2.4 g
- Cholesterol 110 mg
- Sodium 941 mg
- Total Carbs 30.1 g
- Fiber 0.9 g
- Sugar 1.4 g
- Protein 14.6 g

Barbecued Turkey

Prep Time: 10 minutes
Cooking Time: 30 minutes
Serving: 6

Ingredients

- 1 cup Greek yogurt
- 1/2 cup lemon juice
- 1/3 cup canola oil
- 1/2 cup minced fresh parsley
- 1/2 cup chopped green onions
- 4 garlic cloves, minced
- 4 tablespoons fresh minced dill
- 1 teaspoon dried rosemary, crushed
- 1 teaspoon salt
- 1/2 teaspoon pepper
- 1 - 3 lbs. turkey breast half, bone in

Method:

1. Take the first 10 ingredients in a bowl and mix well.
2. Mix turkey with this marinade in a suitable bowl for seasoning.
3. Cover it to marinate for 8 hours of marination.
4. Prepare and preheat the Ninja Foodi Grill in a High-temperature setting.
5. Once it is preheated, open the lid and place the turkey in the grill.
6. Cover the Ninja Foodi Grill's lid and let it grill on the "Grilling Mode" for 15 minutes.
7. Flip the turkey and continue grilling for another 15 minutes until al dente.
8. Grill until the internal temperature reaches 350 degrees F.
9. Slice and serve.

Nutritional Information per Serving:

- Calories 440
- Total Fat 7.9 g

- Saturated Fat 1.8 g
- Cholesterol 5 mg
- Sodium 581 mg
- Total Carbs 21.8 g
- Sugar 7.1 g
- Fiber 2.6 g
- Protein 37.2 g

Chapter 5: Meat

Chili-Spiced Ribs

Prep Time: 10 minutes
Cooking Time: 58 minutes
Serving: 6

Ingredients

Glaze/Sauce

- ½ cup packed brown sugar
- 1/3 cup ketchup
- ½ cup of soy sauce
- 1/6 cup lemon juice
- 3/4 teaspoons minced fresh gingerroot

Ribs

- 1 ½ teaspoon cumin, ground
- 1 tablespoon paprika powder
- 3 lbs. pork baby back ribs
- 1 tablespoon chili powder
- 1 teaspoon garlic powder
- Salt to taste
- 1 ½ tablespoons sugar, brown

Method:

1. Take the first six ingredients in a suitable bowl and mix well.
2. Rub this mixture over the ribs then covers them to refrigerate for 30 minutes of margination.
3. Prepare and preheat the Ninja Foodi Grill on a High-temperature setting.
4. Once it is preheated, open the lid and place the ribs on the grill.
5. Cover the Ninja Foodi Grill's lid and let it grill on the "Grilling Mode" for 45 minutes until al dente.
6. Flip the ribs after every 10 minutes for even cooking.

7. Meanwhile, prepare the sauce by cooking its ingredients for 8 minutes in a saucepan.
8. Pour this sauce over the grilled ribs in the grill.
9. Grill for another 5 minutes side.
10. Serve.

Nutritional Information per Serving:

- Calories 380
- Total Fat 20 g
- Saturated Fat 5 g
- Cholesterol 151 mg
- Sodium 686 mg
- Total Carbs 33 g
- Fiber 1 g
- Sugar 1.2 g
- Protein 21 g

Beef with Pesto

Prep Time: 10 minutes
Cooking Time: 14 minutes
Serving: 4

Ingredients

- 4 cups penne pasta, uncooked
- 10 oz. fresh baby spinach, chopped
- 4 beef (6 oz.) tenderloin steaks
- 1/2 teaspoon salt
- 1/2 teaspoon pepper
- 4 cups grape tomatoes, halved
- 1/2 cup chopped walnuts
- 2/3 cup pesto
- 1/2 cup crumbled feta cheese

Method:

1. At first, prepared the pasta as per the given instructions on the pack.
2. Drain and rinse, then keep this pasta aside.
3. Now season the tenderloin steaks with salt and pepper.
4. Prepare and preheat the Ninja Foodi Grill on a High-temperature setting.
5. Once it is preheated, open the lid and place the steaks on the grill.
6. Cover the Ninja Foodi Grill's lid and let it grill on the "Grilling Mode" for 7 minutes.
7. Flip the steaks and continue grilling for another 7 minutes
8. Toss the pasta with spinach, tomatoes, walnuts, and pesto in a bowl.
9. Slice the grilled steak and top the salad with the steak.
10. Garnish with cheese.
11. Enjoy.

Nutritional Information per Serving:

- Calories 361
- Total Fat 16.3 g

- Saturated Fat 4.9 g
- Cholesterol 114 mg
- Sodium 515 mg
- Total Carbs 19.3 g
- Fiber 0.1 g
- Sugar 18.2 g
- Protein 33.3 g

Sweet Chipotle Ribs

Prep Time: 10 minutes
Cooking Time: 2 hours 5 minutes
Serving: 6

Ingredients

- 3 lbs. baby back ribs

Sauce/Glaze:

- 1 bottle (11.2 oz.) beer
- 1 tablespoon Dijon mustard
- 1 cup barbecue sauce
- 1/3 cup honey
- 2 teaspoon ground chipotle pepper
- 1 ½ cups ketchup
- ½ small onion, chopped
- 1/4 teaspoon pepper
- 1/8 cup Worcestershire sauce
- 1 tablespoon chipotle in adobo sauce, chopped
- ½ teaspoon salt
- ½ teaspoon garlic powder

Method:

1. First, wrap the ribs in a large foil and keep it aside.
2. Prepare and preheat the Ninja Foodi Grill on Roasting mode with medium temperature setting.
3. Once it is preheated, open the lid and place the wrapped ribs on the grill.
4. Cover the Ninja Foodi Grill's lid and let it roast for 1 ½ hour.
5. Take the rest of the ingredients in a saucepan and cook for 45 minutes on a simmer.
6. Brush the grilled ribs with the prepared sauce generously.
7. Place the ribs back into the grill and continue grilling for 10 minutes per side.
8. Serve.

Nutritional Information per Serving:

- Calories 405
- Total Fat 22.7 g
- Saturated Fat 6.1 g
- Cholesterol 4 mg
- Sodium 227 mg
- Total Carbs 26.1 g
- Fiber 1.4 g
- Sugar 0.9 g
- Protein 45.2 g

Steak with Salsa Verde

Prep Time: 10 minutes
Cooking Time: 18 minutes
Serving: 4

Ingredients

- 2 cups salsa Verde
- 2 beef flank steak, diced
- 1/2 teaspoon salt
- 1/2 teaspoon pepper
- 1 cup fresh cilantro leaves
- 2 ripe avocados, diced
- 2 medium tomatoes, seeded and diced

Method:

1. First, rub the steak with salt and pepper to season well.
2. Prepare and preheat the Ninja Foodi Grill on a High-temperature setting.
3. Once it is preheated, open the lid and place the bread slices in the grill.
4. Cover the Ninja Foodi Grill's lid and let it grill on the "Grilling Mode" for 9 minutes.
5. Flip and grill for another 9 minutes until al dente.
6. During this time, blend salsa with cilantro in a blender jug.
7. Slice the steak and serve with salsa, tomato, and avocado.

Nutritional Information per Serving:

- Calories 545
- Total Fat 36.4 g
- Saturated Fat 10.1 g
- Cholesterol 200 mg
- Sodium 272 mg
- Total Carbs 40.7 g
- Fiber 0.2 g
- Sugar 0.1 g
- Protein 42.5 g

Pork with Salsa

Prep Time: 10 minutes
Cooking Time: 12 minutes
Serving: 6

Ingredients

- 2 lbs. pork tenderloin, ¾ inch slices
- 1/4 cup lime juice
- 2 tablespoons olive oil
- 2 garlic cloves, minced
- 1-1/2 teaspoons ground cumin
- 1-1/2 teaspoons dried oregano
- 1/2 teaspoon pepper

Salsa:

- 1 jalapeno pepper, seeded and chopped
- 1 teaspoon sugar
- 1/3 cup chopped red onion
- 2 tablespoons chopped fresh mint
- 2 tablespoons lime juice
- 4 cups pears, chopped peeled
- 1 tablespoon lime zest, grated
- 1/2 teaspoon pepper

Method:

1. Season the pork with lime juice, cumin, oregano, oil, garlic, and pepper in a suitable bowl.
2. Cover to refrigerate for overnight margination.
3. Prepare and preheat the Ninja Foodi Grill on a High-temperature setting.
4. Once it is preheated, open the lid and place the pork in the grill.
5. Cover the Ninja Foodi Grill's lid and let it grill on the "Grilling Mode" for 6 minutes.
6. Flip the pork and continue grilling for another 6 minutes until al dente.

7. Mix the pear salsa ingredients into a separate bowl.
8. Serve the sliced pork with pear salsa.

Nutritional Information per Serving:

- Calories 695
- Total Fat 17.5 g
- Saturated Fat 4.8 g
- Cholesterol 283 mg
- Sodium 355 mg
- Total Carbs 26.4 g
- Fiber 1.8 g
- Sugar 0.8 g
- Protein 117.4 g

Sweet Ham Kabobs

Prep Time: 10 minutes
Cooking Time: 7 minutes
Serving: 2

Ingredients

- 1/2 can (20 oz.) pineapple chunks
- 1/4 cup orange marmalade
- ½ green pepper, cubed
- 1/2 tablespoon mustard
- 1/8 teaspoon ground cloves
- ½ lb. ham, diced
- ¼ lb. Swiss cheese, diced

Method:

1. Take 2 tablespoons of pineapple from pineapples in a bowl.
2. Add mustard, marmalade, and cloves mix well and keep it aside.
3. Thread the pineapple, green pepper, cheese, and ham over the skewers alternatively.
4. Prepare and preheat the Ninja Foodi Grill on the medium's temperature setting.
5. Once it is preheated, open the lid and place the ham skewers in the grill.
6. Cover the Ninja Foodi Grill's lid and let it grill on the "Grilling Mode" for 7 minutes.
7. Continue rotating the skewers every 2 minutes.
8. Pour the sauce on top and serve.

Nutritional Information per Serving:

- Calories 301
- Total Fat 8.9 g
- Saturated Fat 4.5 g
- Cholesterol 57 mg
- Sodium 340 mg
- Total Carbs 24.7 g
- Fiber 1.2 g
- Sugar 1.3 g
- Protein 15.3 g

Steak & Bread Salad

Prep Time: 10 minutes
Cooking Time: 14 minutes
Serving: 4

Ingredients

- 1 tablespoon mustard
- 2 teaspoons packed brown sugar
- 1/2 teaspoon salt
- 1/2 teaspoon pepper
- 1 cup ranch salad dressing
- 1 beef top sirloin steak, diced
- 2 teaspoons chili powder
- 3 large tomatoes, diced
- 2 cups bread, cubed
- 2 tablespoons olive oil
- 2 tablespoons horseradish, finely grated
- 1 cucumber, chopped
- 1 red onion, thinly sliced

Method:

1. First mix the chili powder with salt, pepper, and brown sugar in a bowl
2. Sauté the bread cubes with oil in a skillet for 10 minutes until golden.
3. Take a small bowl and mix horseradish with mustard and salad dressing.
4. Prepare and preheat the Ninja Foodi Grill on High-temperature setting.
5. Once it is preheated, open the lid and place the Steaks in the grill.
6. Cover the Ninja Foodi Grill's lid and let it grill on the "Grilling Mode" for 4 minutes.
7. Flip the steak and continue grilling for another 4 minutes.
8. Toss the sautéed bread cubes with rest o the ingredients and dressing mix in a salad bowl.
9. Slice the grilled steak and serve on top of the salad.
10. Enjoy.

Nutritional Information per Serving:

- Calories 548
- Total Fat 22.9 g
- Saturated Fat 9 g
- Cholesterol 105 mg
- Sodium 350 mg
- Total Carbs 17.5 g
- Sugar 10.9 g
- Fiber 6.3 g
- Protein 40.1 g

Raspberry Pork Chops

Prep Time: 10 minutes
Cooking Time: 20 minutes
Serving: 2

Ingredients

- ½ chipotle in adobo sauce, chopped
- ¼ cup raspberry preserves, seedless
- 1/4 teaspoon salt
- 2 bone-in pork loin chops

Method:

1. Take a small pan and mix preserves with chipotle pepper sauce on medium heat.
2. Keep ¼ cup of this sauce aside and rub the remaining over the pork.
3. Sprinkle salt over the pork and mix well.
4. Prepare and preheat the Ninja Foodi Grill on High-temperature setting.
5. Once it is preheated, open the lid and place 2 pork chops in the grill.
6. Cover the Ninja Foodi Grill's lid and grill them on the "Grilling Mode" for 5 minutes per side.
7. Serve with the reserved sauce.
8. Enjoy.

Nutritional Information per Serving:

- Calories 609
- Total Fat 50.5 g
- Saturated Fat 11.7 g
- Cholesterol 58 mg
- Sodium 463 mg
- Total Carbs 9.9 g
- Fiber 1.5 g
- Sugar 0.3 g
- Protein 29.3 g

Cheese Burgers

Prep Time: 10 minutes
Cooking Time: 20 minutes
Serving: 2

Ingredients

- ¼ cup shredded cheddar cheese
- 3 tablespoons chili sauce, divided
- ½ tablespoon chili powder
- ½ lb. ground beef

To serve:

- Lettuce leaves, mayonnaise, tomato slices
- 2 hamburger buns, split

Method:

1. First, take all the ingredients for patties in a bowl.
2. Thoroughly mix them together then make 2 of the ½ inch patties out of it.
3. Prepare and preheat the Ninja Foodi Grill in a High-temperature setting.
4. Once it is preheated, open the lid and place 2 patties on the grill.
5. Cover the Ninja Foodi Grill's lid and grill them on the "Grilling Mode" for 5 minutes per side.
6. Serve with buns, lettuce, tomato, and mayonnaise.

Nutritional Information per Serving:

- Calories 537
- Total Fat 19.8 g
- Saturated Fat 1.4 g
- Cholesterol 10 mg
- Sodium 719 mg
- Total Carbs 25.1 g
- Fiber 0.9 g
- Sugar 1.4 g
- Protein 37.8 g

American Burger

Prep Time: 10 minutes
Cooking Time: 20 minutes
Serving: 4

Ingredients

- 1/2 cup bread crumbs
- 1/2 teaspoon pepper
- 1 large egg, whisked
- 1/2 teaspoon salt
- 4 seed hamburger buns, cut in half
- 1-lb. ground beef
- 1 tablespoon olive oil

Method:

1. Take all the ingredients for a burger in a suitable bowl except the oil and the buns.
2. Mix them thoroughly together and make 4 of the ½ inch patties.
3. Brush these patties with olive oil.
4. Prepare and preheat the Ninja Foodi Grill on a High-temperature setting.
5. Once it is preheated, open the lid and place 2 patties in the grill.
6. Cover the Ninja Foodi Grill's lid and grill them on the "Grilling Mode" for 5 minutes per side until al dente.
7. Grill the remaining two patties in the same way.
8. Serve with buns.

Nutritional Information per Serving:

- Calories 301
- Total Fat 15.8 g
- Saturated Fat 2.7 g
- Cholesterol 75 mg
- Sodium 389 mg
- Total Carbs 11.7 g
- Fiber 0.3g
- Sugar 0.1 g
- Protein 28.2 g

Basil Pizzas

Prep Time: 10 minutes
Cooking Time: 17 minutes
Serving: 4

Ingredients

- 4 (4 oz.) Italian sausage, sliced
- 1 cup tomato basil pasta sauce
- 1/2 cup Parmesan cheese, grated
- 4 flatbreads
- 1/4 cup olive oil
- 2 cups mozzarella cheese, shredded
- 1/2 cup fresh basil, thinly sliced

Method:

1. Prepare and preheat the Ninja Foodi Grill on a High-temperature setting.
2. Once it is preheated, open the lid and place the sliced sausages on the grill.
3. Cover the Ninja Foodi Grill's lid and grill them on the "Grilling Mode" for 3 minutes per side.
4. Now grill the flatbreads after rubbing with the oil for 3 minutes per side.
5. Top the bread with sauce, sausages, basil, and cheese.
6. Again, place the bread in the Ninja Foodi Grill and cover the lid.
7. Cook on Baking mode for 5 minutes on low-temperature settings.
8. Slice and serve.

Nutritional Information per Serving:

- Calories 308
- Total Fat 20.5 g
- Saturated Fat 3 g
- Cholesterol 42 mg
- Sodium 688 mg
- Total Carbs 40.3 g
- Sugar 1.4 g
- Fiber 4.3 g
- Protein 49 g

Skewers with Chimichurri

Prep Time: 10 minutes
Cooking Time: 20 minutes
Serving: 6

Ingredients

- 1/3 cup fresh cilantro
- 1/3 cup fresh parsley
- Juice of 1/2 lemon
- 1/3 cup fresh basil
- 1 tablespoon red wine vinegar
- 1 garlic clove, minced
- 1 shallot, minced
- 1/2 teaspoon crushed red pepper flakes
- 1/2 cup olive oil, divided
- Salt to taste
- Freshly ground Black pepper to taste
- 1 red onion, cubed
- 1 red pepper, cubed
- 1 orange pepper, cubed
- 1 yellow pepper, cubed
- 1 1/2 lb. sirloin steak, fat trimmed and diced

Method:

1. First, take basil, parsley, vinegar, lemon juice, red pepper, shallots, garlic, and cilantro in a blender jug.
2. Blend well, then add ¼ cup olive oil, salt, and pepper and mix again.
3. Now thread the steak, peppers, and onion on the skewers.
4. Drizzle salt, black pepper, and remaining oil over the skewers.
5. Prepare and preheat the Ninja Foodi Grill on a High-temperature setting.
6. Once it is preheated, open the lid and place four skewers on the grill.
7. Cover the Ninja Foodi Grill's lid and grill them on the "Grilling Mode" for 5 minutes per side.

8. Grill the skewers in a batch until all are cooked.
9. Serve warm with green sauce.

Nutritional Information per Serving:

- Calories 231
- Total Fat 20.1 g
- Saturated Fat 2.4 g
- Cholesterol 110 mg
- Sodium 941 mg
- Total Carbs 20.1 g
- Fiber 0.9 g
- Sugar 1.4 g
- Protein 14.6 g

Lamb Skewers

Prep Time: 10 minutes
Cooking Time: 16 minutes
Serving: 8

Ingredients

- 2 garlic cloves, minced
- 1 10 oz. pack couscous
- 1 tablespoon and 1 teaspoon cumin
- Juice of 2 lemons
- 1 1/2 cup yogurt
- Salt to taste
- 1 1/2 lb. lamb leg, boneless, cubed
- Freshly ground black pepper to taste
- 2 tomatoes, seeded and diced
- 1/2 small red onion, finely chopped
- 3 tablespoon olive oil
- 1/2 cucumber, seeded, and diced
- 1/4 cup finely chopped fresh parsley
- 1/4 cup finely chopped fresh mint
- Lemon wedges, to serve

Method:

1. First, cook the couscous as per the given instructions on the package then fluff with a fork.
2. Whisk yogurt with garlic, cumin, lemon juice, salt, and black pepper in a large bowl.
3. Add lamb and mix well to coat the meat.
4. Separately toss red onion with cucumber, tomatoes, parsley, mint, lemon juice, olive oil, salt, and couscous in salad bowl.
5. Thread the seasoned lamb on 8 skewers and drizzle salt and black pepper over them.
6. Prepare and preheat the Ninja Foodi Grill in a High-temperature setting.

7. Once it is preheated, open the lid and place 4 lamb skewers on the grill.
8. Cover the Ninja Foodi Grill's lid and grill them on the "Grilling Mode" for 4 minutes per side.
9. Cook the remaining skewers in a similar way.
10. Serve warm with prepared couscous.

Nutritional Information per Serving:

- Calories 472
- Total Fat 11.1 g
- Saturated Fat 5.8 g
- Cholesterol 610 mg
- Sodium 749 mg
- Total Carbs 19.9 g
- Fiber 0.2 g
- Sugar 0.2 g
- Protein 13.5 g

Korean Flank Steak

Prep Time: 10 minutes
Cooking Time: 12 minutes
Serving: 4

Ingredients

- 1 teaspoon red pepper flakes
- 1/2 cup and 1 tablespoon soy sauce
- 1 1/2 lb. flank steak
- 1/4 cup and 2 tablespoon vegetable oil
- 1/2 cup rice wine vinegar
- 3 tablespoon Sriracha
- 2 cucumbers, seeded and sliced
- 4 cloves garlic, minced
- 2 tablespoon freshly minced ginger
- 2 tablespoon honey
- 3 tablespoon sesame oil
- 1 teaspoon sugar
- Salt to taste

Method:

1. Mix ½ cup soy sauce, half of the rice wine, honey, ginger, garlic, 2 tablespoon Sriracha sauce, 2 tablespoon sesame oil, and vegetable oil in a large bowl.
2. Pour half of this sauce over the steak and rub it well.
3. Cover the steak and marinate for 10 minutes.
4. For salad mix remaining rice wine vinegar, sesame oil, sugar, red pepper flakes, Sriracha sauce, soy sauce, and salt in a salad bowl.
5. Prepare and preheat the Ninja Foodi Grill on High-temperature setting.
6. Once it is preheated, open the lid and place the steak in the grill.
7. Cover the Ninja Foodi Grill's lid and let it grill on the "Grilling Mode" for 6 minutes per side.
8. Slice and serve with cucumber salad.

Nutritional Information per Serving:

- Calories 327
- Total Fat 3.5 g
- Saturated Fat 0.5 g
- Cholesterol 162 mg
- Sodium 142 mg
- Total Carbs 33.6 g
- Fiber 0.4 g
- Sugar 0.5 g
- Protein 24.5 g

Fajita Skewers

Prep Time: 10 minutes
Cooking Time: 14 minutes
Serving: 8

Ingredients

- 1 bunch scallions, cut into large pieces
- 4 large bell peppers, cubed
- 1 lb. sirloin steak, cubed
- olive oil, for drizzling
- 1 pack tortillas, torn
- Salt to taste
- Ground black pepper to taste

Method:

1. Thread the steak, tortillas, peppers, and scallions on the skewers.
2. Drizzle salt, black pepper, and olive oil over the skewers.
3. Prepare and preheat the Ninja Foodi Grill on the medium temperature setting.
4. Once it is preheated, open the lid and place 4 skewers on the grill.
5. Cover the Ninja Foodi Grill's lid and grill them on the "Grilling Mode" for 7 minutes.
6. Continue rotating the skewers every 2 minutes.
7. Cook the skewers in batches until all are grilled.
8. Serve warm.

Nutritional Information per Serving:

- Calories 353
- Total Fat 7.5 g
- Saturated Fat 1.1 g
- Cholesterol 20 mg
- Sodium 297 mg
- Total Carbs 10.4 g
- Fiber 0.2 g
- Sugar 0.1 g
- Protein 13.1 g

Chapter 6: Fish and Seafood

Shrimp & Tomatoes

Prep Time: 10 minutes
Cooking Time: 8 minutes
Serving: 4

Ingredients

- 1/4 cup yogurt
- 2 teaspoons milk
- 2/3 cup fresh arugula
- 1/3 cup lemon juice
- 2 tablespoons olive oil
- 1/2 teaspoon salt
- 1/2 teaspoon grated lemon zest
- 1-lb. shrimp, peeled and deveined
- 2 green onions, sliced
- 1 teaspoon cider vinegar
- 1/4 teaspoon pepper
- 1 teaspoon Dijon mustard
- 2 garlic cloves, minced
- 1/2 teaspoon sugar
- 12 cherry tomatoes

Method:

1. Season the shrimp with lemon juice, lemon zest, oil, and garlic in a suitable bowl.
2. Let it for 10 minutes of margination.
3. Now arugula, yogurt, milk, green onion, sugar, vinegar, mustard, and ¼ teaspoon salt in a blender.
4. Thread the seasoned shrimp and tomatoes on the skewers alternately.
5. And season the skewers with salt and black pepper.
6. Prepare and preheat the Ninja Foodi Grill on medium-temperature setting.
7. Once it is preheated, open the lid and place the skewers on the grill.

8. Cover the Ninja Foodi Grill's lid and let them grill on the "Grilling Mode" for 2 minutes per side.
9. Cook the shrimp in batches.
10. Serve with the prepared sauce.

Nutritional Information per Serving:

- Calories 338
- Total Fat 3.8 g
- Saturated Fat 0.7 g
- Cholesterol 22 mg
- Sodium 620 mg
- Total Carbs 28.3 g
- Fiber 2.4 g
- Sugar 1.2 g
- Protein 15.4 g

Ginger Lime Salmon

Prep Time: 10 minutes
Cooking Time: 40 minutes
Serving: 5

Ingredients

- 1/4 teaspoon salt
- 1 tablespoon rice vinegar
- 2 teaspoons sugar
- ½ tablespoon grated lime zest
- 1 tablespoon olive oil
- 1/4 teaspoon ground coriander
- 1/4 teaspoon ground pepper
- 1/8 cup lime juice
- 1 cucumber, peeled and chopped
- 1/6 cup chopped fresh cilantro
- 1 garlic clove, minced
- ½ tablespoon finely chopped onion
- 1 teaspoon minced fresh ginger root

Salmon:

- 5 (6 oz.) salmon fillets
- 1/4 teaspoon freshly ground pepper
- ½ tablespoon lime juice
- 1/2 tablespoon olive oil
- 1/6 cup gingerroot, minced
- 1/4 teaspoon salt

Method:

1. Start by blending the first 13 ingredients in a blender until smooth.
2. Season the salmon fillets with ginger, oil, salt, black pepper, lime juice.
3. Prepare and preheat the Ninja Foodi Grill on medium-temperature setting.
4. Once it is preheated, open the lid and place 2 salmon fillets in the grill.

5. Cover the Ninja Foodi Grill's lid and grill them on the "Grilling Mode" for 4 minutes per side.
6. Cook the remaining fillets in a similar way.
7. Serve with the prepared sauce.

Nutritional Information per Serving:

- Calories 457
- Total Fat 19.1 g
- Saturated Fat 11 g
- Cholesterol 262 mg
- Sodium 557 mg
- Total Carbs 18.9 g
- Sugar 1.2 g
- Fiber 1.7 g
- Protein 32.5 g

Pistachio Pesto Shrimp

Prep Time: 10 minutes
Cooking Time: 12 minutes
Serving: 4

Ingredients

- 2 tablespoons lemon juice
- 3/4 cup fresh arugula
- 1/2 cup fresh parsley, minced
- 1/3 cup pistachios, shelled
- 1 garlic clove, peeled
- 1/4 teaspoon grated lemon zest
- 1/2 cup olive oil
- 1 ½ lbs. uncooked shrimp, peeled and deveined
- 1/4 cup Parmesan cheese, shredded
- 1/4 teaspoon salt
- 1/8 teaspoon pepper

Method:

1. Start by adding the first 6 ingredients in a blender until smooth.
2. Add salt, pepper, Parmesan cheese, and mix well.
3. Toss in shrimp and mix well, then cover to refrigerate for 30 minutes.
4. Thread these shrimps on the skewers.
5. Prepare and preheat the Ninja Foodi Grill on the medium temperature setting.
6. Once it is preheated, open the lid and place the skewers on the grill.
7. Cover the Ninja Foodi Grill's lid and grill them on the "Grilling Mode" for 6 minutes.
8. Continue rotating skewers after every 2 minutes.
9. Cook the skewers in batches.
10. Serve.

Nutritional Information per Serving:

- Calories 293

- Total Fat 16 g
- Saturated Fat 2.3 g
- Cholesterol 75 mg
- Sodium 386 mg
- Total Carbs 5.2 g
- Sugar 2.6 g
- Fiber 1.9 g
- Protein 34.2 g

Lemony Garlic Salmon

Prep Time: 10 minutes
Cooking Time: 12 minutes
Serving: 2

Ingredients

- 1/4 teaspoon salt
- 1/4 teaspoon minced fresh rosemary
- 1/4 teaspoon pepper
- 1 garlic clove, minced
- 1 teaspoon grated lemon zest
- 2 salmon fillets (6 oz.)

Method:

1. Take the first five ingredients in a bowl and mix well.
2. Leave the mixture for 15 minutes then rub the salmon with this mixture.
3. Prepare and preheat the Ninja Foodi Grill on a medium-temperature setting.
4. Once it is preheated, open the lid and place 2 salmon fillets on the grill.
5. Cover the Ninja Foodi Grill's lid and grill them on the "Grilling Mode" for 6 minutes.
6. Flip the salmon fillets after 3 minutes.
7. Serve warm.

Nutritional Information per Serving:

- Calories 246
- Total Fat 7.4 g
- Saturated Fat 4.6 g
- Cholesterol 105 mg
- Sodium 353 mg
- Total Carbs 19.4 g
- Sugar 6.5 g
- Fiber 2.7 g
- Protein 37.2 g

Seafood Stuffed Sole

Prep Time: 10 minutes
Cooking Time: 14 minutes
Serving: 2

Ingredients

- 1/4 cup shrimp, chopped, cooked, peeled
- 2 tablespoons butter, melted, divided
- 1/2 can (6 oz.) crabmeat, drained
- 1 tablespoon whipped cream cheese
- 2 tablespoons bread crumbs
- 1 teaspoon minced chive
- 2 (6 oz.) sole fish fillets, cut from a side and insides removed
- 1/4 teaspoon salt
- ½ garlic clove, minced
- ½ teaspoon grated lemon zest
- ½ teaspoon minced fresh parsley
- ¾ cup cherry tomatoes
- 1 tablespoon chicken broth
- 1 tablespoon lemon juice
- 1/4 teaspoon pepper

Method:

1. Thoroughly mix crab with shrimp, cream cheese, chives, lemon zest, garlic, parsley, 2 tablespoon butter, and breadcrumbs in a small bowl.
2. Stuff ¼ of this filling into each fillet and secure the ends with by inserting the toothpicks.
3. Mix tomatoes with salt, pepper, wine, and lemon juice in a separate bowl.
4. Place each stuffed fillet in a foil sheet and top with tomato mixture.
5. Cover and seal the fillets in the foil.
6. Prepare and preheat the Ninja Foodi Grill on the medium temperature setting.
7. Once it is preheated, open the lid and place 2 sealed fillets in the grill.

8. Cover the Ninja Foodi Grill's lid and grill them on the "Grilling Mode" for 7 minutes per side.
9. Serve warm.

Nutritional Information per Serving:

- Calories 248
- Total Fat 15.7 g
- Saturated Fat 2.7 g
- Cholesterol 75 mg
- Sodium 94 mg
- Total Carbs 31.4 g
- Fiber 0.4 g
- Sugar 3.1 g
- Protein 24.9 g

Salmon Lime Burgers

Prep Time: 10 minutes
Cooking Time: 20 minutes
Serving: 2

Ingredients

- 1 tablespoon fresh cilantro, minced
- ½ lb. skinless salmon fillets, cubed
- 1/4 teaspoon salt
- ½ tablespoon soy sauce
- 1/2 tablespoon Dijon mustard
- 1 ½ tablespoons finely chopped shallot
- ½ tablespoon honey
- 1 ½ garlic cloves, minced
- ½ tablespoon grated lime zest
- 1/8 teaspoon pepper
- 2 hamburger buns, cut in half

Method:

1. Thoroughly mix every ingredient for burgers in a bowl except the buns.
2. Make 2 of the ½ inch patties out this mixture.
3. Prepare and preheat the Ninja Foodi Grill on the medium temperature setting.
4. Once it is preheated, open the lid and place 2 patties on the grill.
5. Cover the Ninja Foodi Grill's lid and grill them on the "Grilling Mode" for 5 minutes per side.
6. Serve warm with buns.

Nutritional Information per Serving:

- Calories 408
- Total Fat 21 g
- Saturated Fat 4.3 g
- Cholesterol 150 mg
- Sodium 146 mg
- Total Carbs 21.1 g
- Sugar 0.1 g
- Fiber 0.4 g
- Protein 23 g

Salmon Packets

Prep Time: 10 minutes
Cooking Time: 20 minutes
Serving: 2

Ingredients

- ½ teaspoon lemon-pepper seasoning
- ½ cup carrots, shredded
- 2 (6 oz.) salmon fillets
- 1/4 cup yellow pepper, julienned
- 1/4 cup green pepper, julienned
- 2 teaspoons lemon juice
- 1/4 teaspoon salt
- ½ teaspoon dried parsley flakes
- 1/8 teaspoon pepper

Method:

1. Season the salmon with lemon pepper then place it in a 12-inch square foil sheet.
2. Top the salmon with remaining ingredients then seal the foil.
3. Prepare and preheat the Ninja Foodi Grill on the medium temperature setting.
4. Once it is preheated, open the lid and place 2 fish pockets in the grill.
5. Cover the Ninja Foodi Grill's lid and grill on the "Grilling Mode" for 5 minutes per side.
6. Cook the remaining fillets in a similar way.
7. Serve warm.

Nutritional Information per Serving:

- Calories 351
- Total Fat 4 g
- Saturated Fat 6.3 g
- Cholesterol 360 mg
- Sodium 236 mg
- Total Carbs 19.1 g
- Sugar 0.3 g
- Fiber 0.1 g
- Protein 36 g

Blackened Salmon

Prep Time: 10 minutes
Cooking Time: 10 minutes
Serving: 4

Ingredients

- 2 teaspoons cayenne pepper
- 2 lbs. salmon fillets
- 1 ¼ teaspoon onion salt
- 2 tablespoons lemon pepper
- 2 teaspoons salt
- 6 tablespoons butter, melted
- 3 tablespoons smoked paprika
- 1 teaspoon dry basil
- 1 teaspoon white pepper, ground
- 1 teaspoon black pepper, ground
- 1 teaspoon dry oregano
- 1 teaspoon ancho chili powder
- lemon wedges, to serve
- cooking spray
- dill sprigs, to serve

Method:

1. Liberally season the salmon fillets with butter and other ingredients.
2. Prepare and preheat the Ninja Foodi Grill on the medium temperature setting.
3. Once it is preheated, open the lid and place the fish pockets in the grill.
4. Cover the Ninja Foodi Grill's lid and grill on the "Grilling Mode" for 5 minutes per side.
5. Serve warm.

Nutritional Information per Serving:

- Calories 378
- Total Fat 7 g

- Saturated Fat 8.1 g
- Cholesterol 230 mg
- Sodium 316 mg
- Total Carbs 16.2 g
- Sugar 0.2 g
- Fiber 0.3 g
- Protein 26 g

Chapter 7: Vegetables

Vegetable Orzo Salad

Prep Time: 10 minutes
Cooking Time: 14 minutes
Serving: 2

Ingredients

- 2/3 cups orzo, uncooked
- 1/4-lb. fresh asparagus, trimmed
- 1 small zucchini, sliced
- 1 small sweet yellow, halved
- 1 small portobello mushroom, stem removed
- 1/2 small red onion, halved

Salad:

- 1/4 teaspoon salt
- ½ cup grape tomatoes, halved
- ½ tablespoon minced fresh parsley
- ½ tablespoon minced fresh basil
- 1/8 teaspoon pepper
- ½ cup (2 oz.) crumbled feta cheese

Salad dressing

- 2 garlic cloves, minced
- 1 tablespoon olive oil
- 2 tablespoons balsamic vinegar
- 1 ½ tablespoons lemon juice
- ½ teaspoon lemon-pepper seasoning

Method:

1. Cook the orzo as per the given instructions on the package then drain.
2. Toss all the salad and dressing ingredients in a bowl until well coated.

3. Prepare and preheat the Ninja Foodi Grill on the medium temperature setting.
4. Once it is preheated, open the lid and place the mushrooms, pepper, and onion in grill.
5. Cover the Ninja Foodi Grill's lid and grill them on the "Grilling Mode" for 5 minutes per side.
6. Now grill zucchini and asparagus for 2 minutes per side.
7. Dice the grilled veggies and add them to the salad bowl.
8. Mix well, then stir in orzo.
9. Give it a toss then serve.

Nutritional Information per Serving:

- Calories 246
- Total Fat 14.8 g
- Saturated Fat 0.7 g
- Cholesterol 22 mg
- Sodium 220 mg
- Total Carbs 40.3 g
- Fiber 2.4 g
- Sugar 1.2 g
- Protein 12.4 g

Southwestern Potato Salad

Prep Time: 10 minutes
Cooking Time: 29 minutes
Serving: 4

Ingredients

- 1/2 cup milk
- 1/4 teaspoon cayenne pepper
- 2 poblano peppers
- 1 teaspoon ground cumin
- 1 1/2 lbs. red potatoes, quartered
- 3 tablespoons olive oil
- 1 tablespoon fresh cilantro, minced
- 2 sweet corn ears, without husks
- 1/2 cup sour cream
- 1 tablespoon lime juice
- 1 jalapeno pepper, seeded and minced
- 1 ½ teaspoons garlic salt

Method:

1. Add water and potatoes to a large saucepan and cook or 5 minutes on a boil.
2. Drain and rub the potatoes with oil.
3. Prepare and preheat the Ninja Foodi Grill on the medium temperature setting.
4. Once it is preheated, open the lid and place the poblanos in the grill.
5. Cover the Ninja Foodi Grill's lid and grill on the "Grilling Mode" for 5 minutes per side.
6. Now grill potatoes and corn for 7 minutes per side.
7. Peel the pepper and chop them.
8. Cut corn and potatoes as well and mix well peppers in a bowl.
9. Whisk the rest of the ingredients in a separate bowl then add to the potatoes.
10. Mix well and serve.

Nutritional Information per Serving:

- Calories 338
- Total Fat 3.8 g
- Saturated Fat 0.7 g
- Cholesterol 22 mg
- Sodium 620 mg
- Total Carbs 58.3 g
- Fiber 2.4 g
- Sugar 1.2 g
- Protein 5.4 g

Apple Salad

Prep Time: 10 minutes
Cooking Time: 6 minutes
Serving: 2

Ingredients

- 2 tablespoons orange juice
- 3 tablespoons avocado oil
- 1/4 teaspoon Sriracha chili sauce
- 2 tablespoons fresh cilantro, chopped
- 2 tablespoons vinegar
- ½ garlic clove, minced
- 1 tablespoon honey
- 1/4 teaspoon salt
- 1/4 cup crumbled blue cheese
- 1 apple, wedged
- ½ pack (5 oz.) salad greens

Method:

1. Whisk the first 8 ingredients in a bowl and add ¼ cup of this dressing to the apples.
2. Toss well and let them sit for 10 minutes.
3. Prepare and preheat the Ninja Foodi Grill on the medium temperature setting.
4. Once it is preheated, open the lid and place the apples in the grill.
5. Cover the Ninja Foodi Grill's lid and grill on the "Grilling Mode" for 3 minutes per side.
6. Toss the rest of the salad ingredients together in a salad bowl.
7. Add grilled apples and serve.

Nutritional Information per Serving:

- Calories 438
- Total Fat 4.8 g
- Saturated Fat 1.7 g
- Cholesterol 12 mg
- Sodium 520 mg
- Total Carbs 58.3 g
- Fiber 2.3 g
- Sugar 1.2 g
- Protein 2.1 g

Potatoes in a Foil

Prep Time: 10 minutes
Cooking Time: 15 minutes
Serving: 2

Ingredients

- 2 slices cheddar cheese
- 1 small onion, finely chopped
- 2 ½ bacon strips, crispy and crumbled
- Sour cream, to serve
- 2 tablespoons butter, melted
- 1 ¼ lbs. potatoes, peeled and sliced
- ¼ teaspoon salt
- 1/8 teaspoon pepper

Method:

1. Toss potatoes with salt, pepper, butter, bacon, and onion.
2. Add this mixture to a suitably sized foil sheet and wrap it well to seal.
3. Prepare and preheat the Ninja Foodi Grill in a High-temperature setting.
4. Once it is preheated, open the lid and place the potato pockets in the grill.
5. Cover the Ninja Foodi Grill's lid and grill on the "Grilling Mode" for 15 minutes.
6. Drizzle cheese over hot potatoes.
7. Serve warm.

Nutritional Information per Serving:

- Calories 378
- Total Fat 3.8 g
- Saturated Fat 0.7 g
- Cholesterol 2 mg
- Sodium 620 mg
- Total Carbs 13.3 g
- Fiber 2.4 g
- Sugar 1.2 g
- Protein 5.4 g

Cajun Green Beans

Prep Time: 10 minutes
Cooking Time: 11 minutes
Serving: 2

Ingredients

- ½ lb. fresh green beans, trimmed
- 1/4 teaspoon Cajun seasoning
- ½ tablespoon butter

Method:

1. Add green beans to an 18-inch square sheet.
2. Drizzle Cajun seasoning and butter on top.
3. Cover and seal the foil over the green beans.
4. Prepare and preheat the Ninja Foodi Grill on the medium temperature setting.
5. Once it is preheated, open the lid and place the green bean pockets in the grill.
6. Cover the Ninja Foodi Grill's lid and grill on the "Grilling Mode" for 11 minutes.
7. Serve warm

Nutritional Information per Serving:

- Calories 304
- Total Fat 30.6 g
- Saturated Fat 13.1 g
- Cholesterol 131 mg
- Sodium 834 mg
- Total Carbs 21.4 g
- Fiber 0.2 g
- Sugar 0.3 g
- Protein 4.6 g

Grilled Veggies with Vinaigrette

Prep Time: 10 minutes
Cooking Time: 20 minutes
Serving: 8

Ingredients

Vinaigrette:

- 2 tablespoon Dijon mustard
- 1/2 cup red wine vinegar
- 2 tablespoon honey
- 1 teaspoon salt
- 1/4 teaspoon pepper
- 1/2 cup avocado oil
- 1/2 cup olive oil

Vegetables:

- 4 zucchinis, cut in half
- 2 bunches green onions, trimmed
- 4 yellow squash, cut in half
- 4 sweet onions, wedged
- 4 red peppers, seeded and cut in half
- Cooking spray

Method:

1. Start by whisking the first 5 ingredients in a small bowl.
2. Gradually add oil while mixing the vinaigrette thoroughly.
3. Prepare and preheat the Ninja Foodi Grill on the medium temperature setting.
4. Once it is preheated, open the lid and place the onion quarters in the grill.
5. Cover the Ninja Foodi Grill's lid and grill on the "Grilling Mode" for 5 minutes per side.
6. Grill squash, peppers, and zucchini for 7 minutes per side in the same grill.
7. Finally, grill the green onions for 1 minute per side.
8. Dice the grilled veggies and mix with vinaigrette.

9. Serve.

Nutritional Information per Serving:

- Calories 341
- Total Fat 4 g
- Saturated Fat 0.5 g
- Cholesterol 69 mg
- Sodium 547 mg
- Total Carbs 36.4 g
- Fiber 1.2 g
- Sugar 1 g
- Protein 10.3 g

Grilled Potato

Prep Time: 10 minutes
Cooking Time: 14 minutes
Serving: 2

Ingredients

- 2 tablespoons butter, melted
- 2 potatoes, baked and sliced
- 1/8 teaspoon salt
- 1/8 teaspoon pepper
- ½ cup sour cream
- ¾ cup cheddar cheese, shredded
- 4 bacon slices, crispy and crumbled
- 1 ½ tablespoons chives, minced

Method:

1. First, cut the potatoes into 1-inch thick rounds.
2. Rub them with butter, salt, and black pepper.
3. Prepare and preheat the Ninja Foodi Grill on the medium temperature setting.
4. Once it is preheated, open the lid and place the potatoes slices on the grill.
5. Cover the Ninja Foodi Grill's lid and grill on the "Grilling Mode" for 7 minutes per side.
6. Serve warm with bacon, chives, and sour cream on top.
7. Enjoy.

Nutritional Information per Serving:

- Calories 418
- Total Fat 15.7 g
- Saturated Fat 2.7 g
- Cholesterol 75 mg
- Sodium 94 mg
- Total Carbs 40.4 g
- Fiber 0.1 g
- Sugar 0.3 g
- Protein 4.9 g

Mediterranean Grilled Pizzas

Prep Time: 10 minutes
Cooking Time: 36 minutes
Serving: 4

Ingredients

- 4 tortillas
- 1 ½ tablespoons olive oil

Pizza topping:

- 1/4 cup tomato, chopped
- ½ pack (7 oz.) hummus
- 2 tablespoons olives. sliced
- 1/4 cup feta cheese, crumbled
- 2 tablespoons green onions, thinly sliced

Method:

1. First, brush the tortilla with oil for grilling.
2. Prepare and preheat the Ninja Foodi Grill on the medium temperature setting.
3. Once it is preheated, open the lid and place a tortilla in the grill.
4. Cover the Ninja Foodi Grill's lid and grill on the "Grilling Mode" for 2 minutes per side.
5. Grill the remaining tortillas in the grill in a similar way.
6. Spread the pizza topping over each tortilla and cover the lid again.
7. Cook on Bake Mode at medium temperature settings for 5 minutes.
8. Serve.

Nutritional Information per Serving:

- Calories 391
- Total Fat 12.2 g
- Saturated Fat 2.4 g
- Cholesterol 110 mg
- Sodium 276 mg
- Total Carbs 15 g
- Fiber 0.9 g
- Sugar 1.4 g
- Protein 8.8 g

Chapter 8: Snacks

Cob with Pepper Butter

Prep Time: 10 minutes
Cooking Time: 30 minutes
Serving: 8

Ingredients

- 8 medium ears sweet corn
- 1 cup butter, softened
- 2 tablespoons lemon-pepper seasoning

Method:

1. Season the corn cob with butter and lemon pepper liberally.
2. Prepare and preheat the Ninja Foodi Grill on a medium-temperature setting.
3. Once it is preheated, open the lid and place the corn cob in the grill.
4. Cover the Ninja Foodi Grill's lid and grill on the "Grilling Mode" for 15 minutes while rotating after every 5 minutes.
5. Grill the corn cobs in batches.
6. Serve warm.

Nutritional Information per Serving:

- Calories 148
- Total Fat 22.4 g
- Saturated Fat 10.1 g
- Cholesterol 320 mg
- Sodium 350 mg
- Total Carbs 32.2 g
- Fiber 0.7 g
- Sugar 0.7 g
- Protein 4.3 g

Grilled Eggplant

Prep Time: 10 minutes
Cooking Time: 10 minutes
Serving: 4

Ingredients

- 2 small eggplants, half-inch slices
- 1/4 cup olive oil
- 2 tablespoons lime juice
- 3 teaspoons Cajun seasoning

Method:

1. Liberally season the eggplant slices with oil, lemon juice, and Cajun seasoning.
2. Prepare and preheat the Ninja Foodi Grill on the medium temperature setting.
3. Once it is preheated, open the lid and place the eggplant slices in the grill.
4. Cover the Ninja Foodi Grill's lid and grill on the "Grilling Mode" for 5 minutes per side.
5. Serve.

Nutritional Information per Serving:

- Calories 372
- Total Fat 11.1 g
- Saturated Fat 5.8 g
- Cholesterol 610 mg
- Sodium 749 mg
- Total Carbs 16.9 g
- Fiber 0.2 g
- Sugar 0.2 g
- Protein 13.5 g

Tarragon Asparagus

Prep Time: 10 minutes
Cooking Time: 16 minutes
Serving: 4

Ingredients

- 2 lbs. fresh asparagus, trimmed
- 2 tablespoons olive oil
- 1 teaspoon salt
- 1/2 teaspoon pepper
- 1/4 cup honey
- 4 tablespoons minced fresh tarragon

Method:

1. Liberally season the asparagus by tossing with oil, salt, pepper, honey, and tarragon.
2. Prepare and preheat the Ninja Foodi Grill on the medium temperature setting.
3. Once it is preheated, open the lid and place the asparagus on the grill.
4. Cover the Ninja Foodi Grill's lid and grill on the "Grilling Mode" for 8 minutes per side, give them a toss after 4 minutes.
5. Serve warm.

Nutritional Information per Serving:

- Calories 248
- Total Fat 15.7 g
- Saturated Fat 2.7 g
- Cholesterol 75 mg
- Sodium 94 mg
- Total Carbs 31.4 g
- Fiber 0.6 g
- Sugar 15 g
- Protein 14.1 g

Grilled Butternut Squash

Prep Time: 10 minutes
Cooking Time: 16 minutes
Serving: 4

Ingredients

- 1 medium butternut squash
- 1 tablespoon olive oil
- 1 ½ teaspoons dried oregano
- 1 teaspoon dried thyme
- 1/2 teaspoon salt
- 1/4 teaspoon pepper

Method:

1. Peel and slice the squash into ½ inch thick slices.
2. Remove the center of the slices to discard the seeds.
3. Toss the squash slices with remaining ingredients in a bowl.
4. Prepare and preheat the Ninja Foodi Grill on the medium temperature setting.
5. Once it is preheated, open the lid and place the squash in the grill.
6. Cover the Ninja Foodi Grill's lid and grill on the "Grilling Mode" for 8 minutes per side.
7. Serve warm.

Nutritional Information per Serving:

- Calories 249
- Total Fat 11.9 g
- Saturated Fat 1.7 g
- Cholesterol 78 mg
- Sodium 79 mg
- Total Carbs 41.8 g
- Fiber 1.1 g
- Sugar 20.3 g
- Protein 15 g

Honey Glazed Bratwurst

Prep Time: 10 minutes
Cooking Time: 10 minutes
Serving: 4

Ingredients

- 4 bratwurst links, uncooked
- 1/4 cup Dijon mustard
- 1/4 cup honey
- 2 tablespoons mayonnaise
- 1 teaspoon steak sauce
- 4 brat buns, split

Method:

1. First, mix the mustard with steak sauce and mayonnaise in a bowl.
2. Prepare and preheat the Ninja Foodi Grill on a High-temperature setting.
3. Once it is preheated, open the lid and place the bratwurst on the grill.
4. Cover the Ninja Foodi Grill's lid and grill on the "Grilling Mode" for 10 minutes per side until their internal temperature reaches 320 degrees F.
5. Serve with buns and mustard sauce on top.

Nutritional Information per Serving:

- Calories 213
- Total Fat 14 g
- Saturated Fat 8 g
- Cholesterol 81 mg
- Sodium 162 mg
- Total Carbs 53 g
- Fiber 0.7 g
- Sugar 19 g
- Protein 12 g

Chicken Salad with Blueberry Vinaigrette

Prep Time: 10 minutes
Cooking Time: 14 minutes
Serving: 4

Ingredients

- 2 boneless skinless chicken breasts, halves
- 1 tablespoon olive oil
- 1 garlic clove, minced
- 1/4 teaspoon salt
- 1/4 teaspoon pepper

Vinaigrette:

- 1/4 cup olive oil
- 1/4 cup blueberry preserves
- 2 tablespoons balsamic vinegar
- 2 tablespoons maple syrup
- 1/4 teaspoon ground mustard
- 1/8 teaspoon salt
- Dash pepper

Salads:

- 1 package (10 oz.) salad greens
- 1 cup fresh blueberries
- 1/2 cup canned oranges
- 1 cup crumbled goat cheese

Method:

1. First season the chicken liberally with garlic, salt, pepper and oil in a bowl.
2. Cover to refrigerate for 30 minutes margination.
3. Prepare and preheat the Ninja Foodi Grill on the medium temperature setting.
4. Once it is preheated, open the lid and place the chicken in the grill.

5. Cover the Ninja Foodi Grill's lid and grill on the "Grilling Mode" for 5-7 minutes per side until the internal temperature reaches 330 degrees F.
6. Toss the remaining ingredients for salad and vinaigrette in a bowl.
7. Slice the grilled chicken and serve with salad.

Nutritional Information per Serving:

- Calories 379
- Total Fat 29.7 g
- Saturated Fat 18.6 g
- Cholesterol 141 mg
- Sodium 193 mg
- Total Carbs 23.7g
- Fiber 0.9 g
- Sugar 19.3 g
- Protein 5.2 g

Pineapple with Cream Cheese Dip

Prep Time: 10 minutes
Cooking Time: 8 minutes
Serving: 4

Ingredients

DIP:

- 3 oz. cream cheese, softened
- 1/4 cup yogurt
- 2 tablespoons honey
- 1 tablespoon brown sugar
- 1 tablespoon lime juice
- 1 teaspoon grated lime zest

Pineapple

- 1 fresh pineapple
- 1/4 cup packed brown sugar
- 3 tablespoons honey
- 2 tablespoons lime juice

Method:

1. First, slice the peeled pineapple into 8 wedges then cut each wedge into 2 spears.
2. Toss the pineapple with sugar, lime juice, and honey in a bowl then refrigerate for 1 hour.
3. Meanwhile, prepare the lime dip by whisking all its ingredients together in a bowl.
4. Remove the pineapple from its marinade.
5. Prepare and preheat the Ninja Foodi Grill on the medium temperature setting.
6. Once it is preheated, open the lid and place the pineapple on the grill.
7. Cover the Ninja Foodi Grill's lid and grill on the "Grilling Mode" for 4 minutes per side.
8. Serve with lime dip.

Nutritional Information per Serving:

- Calories 368
- Total Fat 6 g
- Saturated Fat 1.2 g
- Cholesterol 351 mg
- Sodium 103 mg
- Total Carbs 72.8 g
- Fiber 9.2 g
- Sugar 32.9 g
- Protein 7.2 g

Ninja Grill Hot Dogs

Prep Time: 10 minutes
Cooking Time: 12 minutes
Serving: 4

Ingredients

- 1 cup cabbage slaw
- 4 hot dogs
- 4 bacon slices, crispy
- 4 hot dog buns, cut in half
- 1/8 cup onion, chopped

Method:

1. Sear the bacon in a skillet until crispy from both the sides.
2. Wrap a bacon strip around each hot dog and secure it by inserting a toothpick.
3. Prepare and preheat the Ninja Foodi Grill in a High-temperature setting.
4. Once it is preheated, open the lid and place 2 hot dogs in the grill.
5. Cover the Ninja Foodi Grill's lid and grill on the "Grilling Mode" for 6 minutes while rotating after every 2 minutes.
6. Cook all the hot dogs in batches then remove the toothpick.
7. Serve warm in a hotdog bun with cabbage slaw and onion.
8. Enjoy.

Nutritional Information per Serving:

- Calories 301
- Total Fat 32.2 g
- Saturated Fat 2.4 g
- Cholesterol 110 mg
- Sodium 276 mg
- Total Carbs 25 g
- Fiber 0.9 g
- Sugar 31.4 g
- Protein 28.8 g

Chapter 9: Desserts

Ban**Ana Butter Kabobs

Prep Time: 10 minutes
Cooking Time: 6 minutes
Serving: 4

Ingredients

- 1 loaf (10 3/4 oz.) cake, cubed
- 2 large bananas, one-inch slices
- 1/4 cup butter, melted
- 2 tablespoons brown sugar
- 1/2 teaspoon vanilla extract
- 1/8 teaspoon ground cinnamon
- 4 cups butter pecan ice cream
- 1/2 cup butterscotch ice cream topping
- 1/2 cup chopped pecans, toasted

Method:

1. Thread the cake and bananas over the skewers alternately.
2. Whisk butter with cinnamon, vanilla, and brown sugar in a small bowl.
3. Brush this mixture over the skewers liberally.
4. Prepare and preheat the Ninja Foodi Grill on the medium temperature setting.
5. Once it is preheated, open the lid and place the banana skewers on the grill.
6. Cover the Ninja Foodi Grill's lid and grill on the "Grilling Mode" for 3 minutes per side.
7. Serve with ice cream, pecan and butterscotch topping on top.

Nutritional Information per Serving:

- Calories 419
- Total Fat 19.7 g
- Saturated Fat 18.6 g
- Cholesterol 141 mg

- Sodium 193 mg
- Total Carbs 23.7 g
- Fiber 0.9 g
- Sugar 19.3 g
- Protein 5.2 g

Fruit Kabobs

Prep Time: 10 minutes
Cooking Time: 8 minutes
Serving: 6

Ingredients

- 1 tablespoon butter
- 1/2 cup apricot preserves
- 1 tablespoon water
- 1/8 teaspoon ground cinnamon
- 1/8 teaspoon ground nutmeg
- 3 nectarines, quartered
- 3 peaches, quartered
- 3 plums, quartered
- 1 loaf (10-3/4 oz.) lb. cake, cubed

Method:

1. Take the first five ingredients in a small saucepan and stir cook for 3 minutes on medium heat.
2. Alternately thread the lb. cake and fruits on the skewers.
3. Brush these skewers with the apricot mixture.
4. Prepare and preheat the Ninja Foodi Grill on the medium temperature setting.
5. Once it is preheated, open the lid and place the skewers on the grill.
6. Cover the Ninja Foodi Grill's lid and grill on the "Grilling Mode" for 2 minutes per side.
7. Cook the skewers in batches.
8. Serve

Nutritional Information per Serving:

- Calories 248
- Total Fat 15.7 g
- Saturated Fat 2.7 g
- Cholesterol 75 mg
- Sodium 94 mg
- Total Carbs 38.4 g
- Fiber 0.3 g
- Sugar 10.1 g
- Protein 14.1 g

Berry Cobbler

Prep Time: 10 minutes
Cooking Time: 20 minutes
Serving: 2

Ingredients

- 2 cans (21 oz.) pie filling, raspberry flavor
- 1-1/4 cups water
- 1/2 cup canola oil
- 1 (8 oz.) package cake mix
- Vanilla ice cream,

Method:

1. First, mix the cake mix with oil and water in a bowl until smooth.
2. Place the foil packet on a working surface and pie filling.
3. Spread the cake mix on top of the filling.
4. Cover the foil packet and seal it.
5. Prepare and preheat the Ninja Foodi Grill on the medium temperature setting.
6. Once it is preheated, open the lid and place the squash in the grill.
7. Cover the Ninja Foodi Grill's lid and cook on Bake Mode for 20 minutes.
8. Serve fresh with vanilla ice cream on top.

Nutritional Information per Serving:

- Calories 319
- Total Fat 11.9 g
- Saturated Fat 1.7 g
- Cholesterol 78 mg
- Sodium 79 mg
- Total Carbs 14.8 g
- Fiber 1.1 g
- Sugar 8.3 g
- Protein 5 g

Marshmallow Roll-Up

Prep Time: 10 minutes
Cooking Time: 10 minutes
Serving: 2

Ingredients

- 1 flour tortilla
- 1 handful mini marshmallows
- 1 handful of chocolate chips
- 2 graham crackers

Method:

1. Spread a 12x12 inch foil on a working surface.
2. Place the tortilla over this sheet and top it with graham crackers, chocolate chips, and marshmallows.
3. Roll the tortilla tightly by rolling the foil sheet.
4. Prepare and preheat the Ninja Foodi Grill on the medium temperature setting.
5. Once it is preheated, open the lid and place the squash in the grill.
6. Cover the Ninja Foodi Grill's lid and grill on the "Grilling Mode" for 5 minutes per side.
7. Unwrap and slice in half.
8. Serve.

Nutritional Information per Serving:

- Calories 495
- Total Fat 17.5 g
- Saturated Fat 4.8 g
- Cholesterol 283 mg
- Sodium 355 mg
- Total Carbs 26.4 g
- Fiber 1.8 g
- Sugar 0.8 g
- Protein 17.4 g

Cinnamon the grilled Peaches

Prep Time: 10 minutes
Cooking Time: 2 minutes
Serving: 4

Ingredients

- 1/4 cup salted butter
- 1 tablespoon 1 teaspoon granulated sugar
- 1/4 teaspoon cinnamon
- 4 ripe peaches, halved and pitted
- vegetable oil

Method:

1. Mix sugar with butter and cinnamon in a bowl until smooth.
2. Prepare and preheat the Ninja Foodi Grill on the medium temperature setting.
3. Once it is preheated, open the lid and place the peaches on the grill.
4. Cover the Ninja Foodi Grill's lid and grill on the "Grilling Mode" for 1 minute per side.
5. Serve the peaches with cinnamon butter on top.
6. Enjoy.

Nutritional Information per Serving:

- Calories 401
- Total Fat 8.9 g
- Saturated Fat 4.5 g
- Cholesterol 57 mg
- Sodium 340 mg
- Total Carbs 54.7 g
- Fiber 1.2 g
- Sugar 1.3 g
- Protein 5.3 g

Rum-Soaked Pineapple

Prep Time: 10 minutes
Cooking Time: 15 minutes
Serving: 6

Ingredients

- 1/2 cup rum
- 1/2 cup packed brown sugar
- 1 teaspoon ground cinnamon
- 1 pineapple, cored and sliced
- cooking spray
- Vanilla ice cream

Method:

1. Mix run with cinnamon and brown sugar in a suitable bowl.
2. Pour this mixture over the pineapple rings and mix well.
3. Let them soak for 15 minutes and flip the pineapples after 7 minutes.
4. Prepare and preheat the Ninja Foodi Grill in a High-temperature setting.
5. Once it is preheated, open the lid and place the pineapple slices on the grill.
6. Cover the Ninja Foodi Grill's lid and grill on the "Grilling Mode" for 4 minutes per side.
7. Serve with ice cream scoop on top.

Nutritional Information per Serving:

- Calories 427
- Total Fat 31.1 g
- Saturated Fat 4.2 g
- Cholesterol 123 mg
- Sodium 86 mg
- Total Carbs 49 g
- Sugar 12.4 g
- Fiber 19.8 g
- Protein 13.5 g

Apricots with Brioche

Prep Time: 10 minutes
Cooking Time: 4 minutes
Serving: 8

Ingredients

- 8 ripe apricots
- 2 tablespoon butter
- 2 tablespoon sugar
- 4 slice brioches, diced
- 2 tablespoon Honey
- 2 cup vanilla ice cream

Method:

1. Toss the apricot halves with butter and sugar.
2. Prepare and preheat the Ninja Foodi Grill on the medium temperature setting.
3. Once it is preheated, open the lid and place brioche slices in the grill.
4. Cover the Ninja Foodi Grill's lid and grill on the "Grilling Mode" for 1 minute per side.
5. Now grill the apricots in the same grill for 1 minute per side.
6. Top these slices with apricot slices, honey, and a scoop of vanilla ice cream.
7. Serve.

Nutritional Information per Serving:

- Calories 398
- Total Fat 13.8 g
- Saturated Fat 5.1 g
- Cholesterol 200 mg
- Sodium 272 mg
- Total Carbs 53.6 g
- Fiber 1 g
- Sugar 1.3 g
- Protein 11.8 g

Marshmallow Stuffed Banana

Prep Time: 10 minutes
Cooking Time: 5 minutes
Serving: 1

Ingredients

- ¼ cup of chocolate chips
- 1 banana
- ¼ cup mini marshmallows

Method:

1. Place a peeled banana over a 12 x 12-inch foil sheet.
2. Make aa slit in the banana lengthwise and stuff this slit with chocolate chips and marshmallows.
3. Wrap the foil around the banana and seal it.
4. Prepare and preheat the Ninja Foodi Grill on the medium temperature setting.
5. Once it is preheated, open the lid and place the banana in the grill.
6. Cover the Ninja Foodi Grill's lid and grill on the "Grilling Mode" for 5 minutes.
7. Unwrap and serve.

Nutritional Information per Serving:

- Calories 372
- Total Fat 11.8 g
- Saturated Fat 4.4 g
- Cholesterol 62 mg
- Sodium 871 mg
- Total Carbs 45.8 g
- Fiber 0.6 g
- Sugar 27.3 g
- Protein 4 g

Chapter 10: 21 Days Meal Plan

Week 01

Day 1

Breakfast: Grilled French Toast

Lunch: Mediterranean Grilled Pizzas

Snack: Tarragon Asparagus

Dinner: Fajita Skewers

Dessert: Fruit Kabobs

Day 2

Breakfast: Sausage with Eggs

Lunch: Grilled Potato Rounds

Snack: Grilled Butternut Squash

Dinner: Korean Flank Steak

Dessert: Berry Cobbler

Day 3

Breakfast: Grilled Chicken Tacos

Lunch: Grilled Veggies with Vinaigrette

Snack: Honey Glazed Bratwurst

Dinner: Lamb Skewers

Dessert: Marshmallow Roll-Up

Day 4

Breakfast: Grilled Bruschetta

Lunch: Cajun Green Beans

Snack: Chicken Salad with Blueberry Vinaigrette

Dinner: Skewers with Chimichurri

Dessert: Cinnamon Grilled Peaches

Day 5

Breakfast: Toast Kebabs

Lunch: Potatoes in a Foil

Snack: Pineapple with Cream Cheese Dip

Dinner: American Burger

Dessert: Rum-Soaked Pineapple

Day 6

Breakfast: Bacon-Herb Grit

Lunch: Apple Salad

Snack: Bacon Hot Dogs

Dinner: Basil Pizzas

Dessert: Apricots with Brioche

Day 7

Breakfast: Coconut French Toast

Lunch: Southwestern Potato Salad

Snack: Cob with Pepper Butter

Dinner: American Burger

Dessert: Marshmallow Stuffed Banana

Week 02

Day 1

Breakfast: Avocado Eggs

Lunch: Vegetable Orzo Salad

Snack: Grilled Eggplant

Dinner: Bratwurst Potatoes

Dessert: Banana Butter Kabobs

Day 2

Breakfast: Bruschetta Portobello Mushrooms

Lunch: Blackened Salmon

Snack: Tarragon Asparagus

Dinner: Cheese Burgers

Dessert: Fruit Kabobs

Day 3

Breakfast: Espresso Glazed Bagels

Lunch: Salmon Packets

Snack: Grilled Butternut Squash

Dinner: Raspberry Pork Chops

Dessert: Berry Cobbler

Day 4

Breakfast: Sausage with Eggs

Lunch: Salmon Lime Burgers

Snack: Honey Glazed Bratwurst

Dinner: Steak & Bread Salad

Dessert: Marshmallow Roll-Up

Day 5

Breakfast: Grilled French Toast

Lunch: Potatoes in a Foil

Snack: Chicken Salad with Blueberry Vinaigrette

Dinner: Sweet Ham Kabobs

Dessert: Cinnamon Grilled Peaches

Day 6

Breakfast: Grilled Chicken Tacos

Lunch: Seafood Stuffed Sole

Snack: Pineapple with Cream Cheese Dip

Dinner: Pork with Salsa

Dessert: Rum-Soaked Pineapple

Day 7

Breakfast: Grilled Bruschetta

Lunch: Lemon-Garlic Salmon

Snack: Bacon Hot Dogs

Dinner: Steak with Salsa Verde

Dessert: Apricots with Brioche

Week 03

Day 1

Breakfast: Grilled French Toast

Lunch: Mediterranean Grilled Pizzas

Snack: Tarragon Asparagus

Dinner: Fajita Skewers

Dessert: Fruit Kabobs

Day 2

Breakfast: Sausage with Eggs

Lunch: Grilled Potato Rounds

Snack: Grilled Butternut Squash

Dinner: Korean Flank Steak

Dessert: Berry Cobbler

Day 3

Breakfast: Grilled Chicken Tacos

Lunch: Grilled Veggies with Vinaigrette

Snack: Honey Glazed Bratwurst

Dinner: Lamb Skewers

Dessert: Marshmallow Roll-Up

Day 4

Breakfast: Grilled Bruschetta

Lunch: Cajun Green Beans

Snack: Chicken Salad with Blueberry Vinaigrette

Dinner: Skewers with Chimichurri

Dessert: Cinnamon Grilled Peaches

Day 5

Breakfast: Toast Kebabs

Lunch: Potatoes in a Foil

Snack: Pineapple with Cream Cheese Dip

Dinner: American Burger

Dessert: Rum-Soaked Pineapple

Day 6

Breakfast: Bacon-Herb Grit

Lunch: Apple Salad

Snack: Bacon Hot Dogs

Dinner: Basil Pizzas

Dessert: Apricots with Brioche

Day 7

Breakfast: Coconut French Toast

Lunch: Southwestern Potato Salad

Snack: Cob with Pepper Butter

Dinner: American Burger

Dessert: Marshmallow Stuffed Banana

Conclusion

Ninja Foodi Grill is nothing but convenience for those who love to enjoy nicely grilled food but too busy to set up an outdoor grill. It has brought innovation right at our fingertips by bringing all the necessary cooking in a digital one-touch device. It is simple to manage and control. And what makes the Ninja foodi grill apart from other electric grills is the diversity of options it provides for cooking all in a single pot. The ceramic coated interior and accessories make grilling an effortless experience. This cookbook puts the idea of electric grill into perspective by discussing the basics of using the Ninja Foodi Grill. The company has launched the appliance with only one aim that is to provide convenient grilling for all. Try the flavorsome grilling recipes in your Ninja Food grills and experience good taste with amazing aroma, all with little efforts and lesser time.